Flower
Crafts
IN A WEEKEND

Flower Crafts

IN A WEEKEND

Exquisite gifts to make using fresh, dried, pressed, silk and parchment flowers

C O R A L   W A L K E R

NH
NEW
HOLLAND

To James

First Published in the UK in 1996 by
New Holland (Publishers) Ltd
24 Nutford Place, London W1H 6DQ

ISBN 1 85368 726 X (hbk)
ISBN 1 85368 727 8 (pbk)

Editor: Emma Callery
Designer: Peter Crump
Photographer: Shona Wood

Editorial Direction: Yvonne McFarlane

Reproduction by Hirt and Carter (Pty) Ltd
Printed and bound by Times Offset (M) Sdn. Bhd.

Acknowledgments
The author would like to thank the following
companies and people:
Ascalon Design Parchment Flowers, The Coach House,
Aylesmore Court, St Briavels, Gloucestershire GL15 6UQ
(01594 530567) who supply a vast range of fabulous
parchment flowers and who kindly supplied us the beautiful
peony roses on page 20 and sunflower on page 29.
Specialist Crafts Ltd, PO Box 247, Leicester LE1 9QS
(0116 251 0405) who supply a wide range of craft materials
and equipment and who were kind enough to give us the card
blanks on page 68.
Prices Patent Candle Co Ltd, 110 York Road, London SW11
3RU (0171 228 2001) for the various candles used
throughout the book.
Also a big thank you to Shona Wood for providing wonderful
lunches throughout the photography, to Jo Ryde for jumping
on the telephone whenever I asked, Karen Keen for enduring
many a late evening, Gill and Yvonne for their support, and
finally my long-suffering family who felt they were living in a
florist's shop at times!

Important:
Every effort has been made to present clear and accurate
instructions. Therefore, the author and publishers can accept
no liability for any injury, illness or damage which may inadver-
tently be caused to the user whilst following these instructions.

CONTENTS

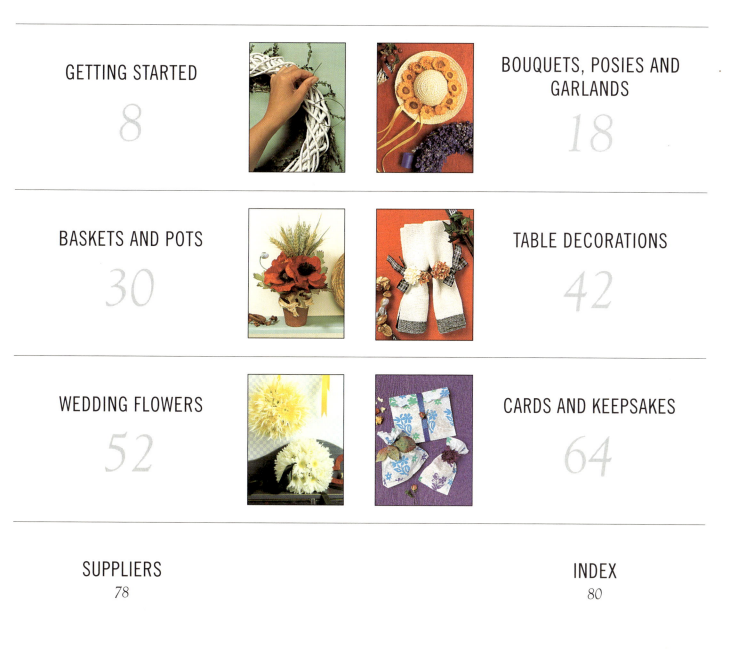

INTRODUCTION

Flowers are probably one of the most frequently given gifts, whether to celebrate, commiserate, congratulate or simply say 'thank you'. It is something of a relief that flowers always come up trumps when you're stuck for a present: they are certain to be appreciated as they always brighten up the home, whatever the season, whatever the reason. But however much a bunch of flowers is well-regarded, it can also be a little uninspired, and in *Flower Crafts*, I have endeavoured to go beyond the standard tenets of flower arranging to show just how imaginative you can be with all things floral. So although you will find some pretty posies and baskets in this book, there is also a host of really exciting and novel ways to present flowers as a gift. I have also tried to include as many different types of flowery things as possible — fresh flowers, yes, but also dried, pressed, silk, plastic and, possibly my favourites, parchment.

It has been the relatively recent development and improvement of artificial flowers and foliage which has been such an inspiration to me. Fake no longer means cheap and nasty. Instead, manufacturers are producing blooms and leaves of startling beauty. Some are very realistic, others are stylized, and they have expanded the floral designer's repertoire considerably.

Floral design is hugely enjoyable, very creative and immensely satisfying. You need only a minimum of skill (the flowers themselves really do the work), experience and equipment. The main criterion is an appreciation of flowers. If you are not able to grow your own, I have included tips on getting the best from fresh flowers, how to help them last as long as possible and how to dry, press or preserve those for other displays.

The projects cover a wealth of ideas from traditional bouquets and baskets, to unusual greetings cards, candles, pots and garlands. Some combine other craft techniques such as papier mâché, stencilling or decoupage, all of which are very rewarding to do if you haven't tried your hand at them before. And there is a whole chapter dedicated to weddings. I hope you will feel confident enough to make some of these particular projects and give them as your own bridal gift.

The projects are all clearly illustrated and easy to follow, but I hope you will be inspired to adapt and develop them as you want, to stamp them with your own style which is the hallmark of a gift that really is that little bit special.

Coral Walker

GETTING STARTED

There are very few hard and fast rules about flower arranging, and if you're looking to create gifts which make use of silk or parchment flowers, you will not have to worry much at all. In this chapter, we look at the principal elements of floral design: fresh flowers and traditional flower arranging techniques, as well as drying, pressing, wiring and other useful floristry tips. Whatever preconceptions you might have, you do not need to spend a lot of money on elaborate equipment, and many of those that are discussed here can be found in any average home.

MATERIALS AND EQUIPMENT

CHICKEN WIRE OR WIRE MESH

This can be bought from any hardware or DIY store in various gauges. Alternatively, you can buy floral wire mesh which is plastic coated and kinder to your hands. The former is cheaper, but you will need to wear gloves to handle it. It can be cut with wirecutters, secateurs or pliers. Use it for making wreath bases, topiary shapes or pendants.

FLORIST'S FOAM

This the mainstay of flower arranging. It is available for fresh flowers (generally green) and for dry arrangements (grey). The foam for fresh flowers must be soaked thoroughly in water before use and sprayed regularly with fresh water to keep the flowers healthy. This type of foam holds a lot of water, so don't just run it under the tap; although it may appear completely wet, it is unlikely to have had the chance to absorb sufficient water.

Florist's foam comes in a variety of different shapes: spheres, rounds and bricks are the most popular, but you can also buy garlands, posy holders and other shapes used by professional florists for funerals or weddings.

Both wet and dry foam can be cut down to any size or shape with a large, dull-bladed knife. Dry foam is quite unpleasant to the touch and it is advisable to wear thin gloves if you have sensitive skin.

FLORIST'S SOFT CLAY

This is rather like soft modelling clay, which does not harden and which can be used for fresh and dry flower arrangements. It is wedged into the base of the container and the flower stems are pushed into it to hold them in place. It is also used to stick pinholders or small prongs to the base of a container.

GLUE GUN

This little electric, trigger-operated hobby gun is perfectly adequate for most floral projects. The glue is inserted as a solid stick into the back of the gun. The glue then melts and can be squeezed on to the item you want to stick. For anyone unfamiliar with a glue gun it is a tremendous asset, as you will no longer need to hold on to two sticky items while waiting for them to adhere. However, the glue is very hot and can burn. The glue also dries very rapidly, so be sure of where you want to place your item first.

PINHOLDERS

These sit at the base of a container and vary from plastic prongs on which florist's foam is impaled, to the spiky metal versions that are used to hold flower stems in place.

SECATEURS AND SCISSORS

Secateurs are really useful for cutting wire as well as pruning the roses: which means that they are very handy if you are planning on using parchment flowers which come on stiff wires. Strong, sharp kitchen scissors are good for just about everything else, although if you want to tackle decoupage (see page 17) you will need a smaller pair.

TAPES

The most common floral tape is gutta percha — a green, white or brown, stretchy tape which is used to bind flower stems together. It is immensely useful and can be called into service whenever any types of flowers need to be bound together. Other floral tapes include an adhesive version for sticking florist's foam to a container and the papery green tape that is used for binding a buttonhole or creating an artificial stem.

WIRE

Florist's wire is sold as stub wire (in various thicknesses or gauges — medium gauge is suitable for most things) and reel wire. The former comes in bunches of cut lengths of wire that are between about 15 and 25 cm (6 and 10 in) long. It is used for numerous floral tasks. An investment in one bunch of medium gauge wires will probably be all you need. Reel wire is thinner and, as you would presume from its name, comes on a reel. It is used really in place of twine or string, or where a fine finish is required (a buttonhole, for example).

German pins are U-shaped pieces of thick wire (rather like old-fashioned hair pins) which are used to secure moss or other items to florist's foam.

FRESH FLOWERS

Always choose the very best flowers, whether you grow your own or buy from a florist. Look for fresh, new blooms with crisp foliage. Avoid flowers or buds which have browning petals or where foliage is drooping or discolouring. Sometimes, although not always, it is worth paying a little extra for the benefits of a good florist shop where the flowers are well cared for and sold in peak condition, rather than the cheaper market stall. Having said that, I have been pleasantly surprised by market flowers, and even those bought by the roadside, and very disappointed with expensive blooms. Conditioning the flowers when they arrive home is probably the best advice, wherever they come from.

CONDITIONING

For cut flowers to last, they must be conditioned. This will enable them to absorb maximum water right up to the flowerheads. Obviously, some varieties last better than others, but all flowers will die quickly unless cared for. If you want long-lasting varieties, try chrysanthemums, carnations, lilies, gypsophila, statice, alstroemeria and golden rod. Varieties with slightly less longevity, but still guaranteed to give you several days life, include: roses

(although hothouse varieties in winter rarely open or last very long), gerberas, tulips, narcissi and delphiniums.

To condition your flowers, first strip away the foliage on the lower part of the stems ①. Any leaves below the waterline will rot, and any rotting matter will encourage bacteria which

will cause the plant to die rapidly. Then cut at least 5 cm (2 in) from the end of the stem with sharp scissors, cutting at an angle ②. With very woody stems, like roses, use a sharp knife to slice up the stem end another 5 cm (2 in). This will ensure maximum water absorption. Place the trimmed flowers into a cool place, in a deep container of water.

Some plants may require a little more assistance. Sunflowers, for example, should be totally immersed in water (lay them in a bath); while tulips and other flowers with hollow stems may develop air bubbles in the stem, causing the plant to droop alarmingly. One way to disperse this is to turn the plant upside down, fill it with water, place your thumb over the end and insert into a container of water ③. If the plant still wilts (tulips are notorious for this), prick a pin through the stem just under the flowerhead.

Once arranged, avoid placing the flowers near fruit. Experts have discovered that ripening fruit (particularly bananas) emits an ether which has a disastrous effect on cut flowers causing them to wilt.

Any flowers arranged in florist's foam will need a daily drink of fresh water, otherwise the foam will dry out and the flowers will die.

DRYING FLOWERS

If you're in a hurry, most florists now stock a range of dried flowers to buy; although the quality will vary from place to place. Always choose freshly-dried specimens and avoid dusty, faded ones. However, with many flowers it is simplicity itself to dry your own. Rows of hanging, drying flowers can also look decorative in themselves, giving an added dimension to a kitchen or utility room.

There are basically three ways to preserve flowers:

AIR DRYING

This is the simplest and works for quite a lot of flowers. Use this method for roses, peonies, hydrangeas, statice, sunflowers, seedheads, helichrysum and

helebores and geraniums can all be dried in this way. You will need to buy silica gel (which is actually crystals), borax or silver sand from a hardware store or chemist. Place the crystals or powder in an airtight container. Lay the flowers on top and gently cover with more crystals/powder ③. Make sure the plants are completely covered. Now cover with a tight-fitting lid and leave. If you are using silica gel, check after two or three days. To test, gently shake back the crystals and touch the petals, they should feel slightly tissuey and leathery. (Some crystals change colour as they absorb moisture, and this will also be an indicator as to when the

sunray (helipterum). Simply bunch a few stems together (not too many, as air should be allowed to circulate between the flowerheads. If the flowerheads are too clustered, they may go mouldy and brown). Wind a rubber band around the end of the stems ① and hang the flowers upside down from a butcher's hook (or similar) on a clothes drying rack, bookcase or shelf in a place well out of sunlight. Avoid steamy areas, or any room which is not warm and completely dry. Sunlight will strip your flowers of all colour really quickly.

Flowers will take up to three weeks before they are dry. To test, turn the flowers back up the right way; the stem should completely support the flowerhead. If it droops even slightly, or feels soft to the touch, the plant isn't quite ready and will need longer.

Hydrangeas and delphiniums can also be dried by standing them upright in a little water. When the water has been absorbed, leave the plants standing where they are until dry.

Dried petals, especially those from roses, make lovely confetti or potpourri. To do this, lay out the petals on some newspaper or brown wrapping paper ②. Cover with another sheet of paper and weight down *gently* with two or three newspapers. After a week, they should be ready to use

DRYING WITH DESICCANTS
Some specimens need to have the moisture drawn from them. Narcissi, camelias, carnations, fuchsias, lilies,

plants are ready). Borax and silver sand will take longer to work — around 10 days or so.

You can speed up this process by placing your container (with silica gel and without the lid) in a microwave oven. Put in a small cup of water beside your container and blast on full power for between 1 and 4 minutes. (Denser blooms will take longer than fragile, single petalled varieties.) If you want to try this method it is worth experimenting as all microwave ovens vary, and so do the plants you use. Time and practice will yield the best results.

PRESERVING WITH GLYCERINE

This is the method used to preserve foliage. Although I haven't used any preserved leaves in this book, it is worth knowing how to do this, as the foliage will last for many, many months (even years) because the glycerine gives the leaves a supple, leathery appearance.

Use late spring or early summertime foliage, when the plant is still taking up water (in autumn, it will stop!). Mix up one part glycerine to two parts very hot water. Allow the solution to cool. Cut the stems at a sharp angle and stand in about 8 cm (3 in) of the cooled glycerine solution. As the plant begins to absorb the glycerine, the leaves will change to a dark, coppery colour. Any glycerine sweat beads which form can be wiped from the leaves. Check every week or so until the leaves have changed colour and are supple and leathery to the touch.

PRESSING FLOWERS

Pressing flowers is a well established hobby. It is a wonderful way to capture the beauty and fragility of a plant without losing any of its colour. It is also a lovely method of preserving wild flowers, which are usually too fragile to last as cut flowers and which generally do not dry well.

Pick flowers around midday when all the dew has evaporated and the plant has taken up sufficient water. Lay gently in a basket and press as soon as possible. If you want to pick wild

flowers, it is worth putting them into a plastic bag which, if you blow up like a balloon, will keep the flowers in a satisfactory state until you return home. You do not need a flower press, although if you enjoy pressing flowers, you will no doubt want to make or buy one as generally they are more manageable and easier to use. Instead, you can use heavy books and layers of tissue paper and cardboard (although with this latter method you will need to affix 'do not touch' notes to prevent unsuspecting members of the household from disturbing the pile!).

Take a piece of tissue paper and lay the flowers or leaves on top, leaving sufficient space around each one. (Multi-petalled flowers will need breaking down into smaller parts for pressing, but single flowers can be pressed whole.) When you have filled the tissue, place another piece on top and put the whole thing in between two pieces of corrugated cardboard (for thicker specimens, it is worth adding a layer of blotting paper as well). Put the whole sandwich in between some heavy books (make sure the books are larger all around so that the flowers on the outer edges are pressed correctly). After a day or so, place another book on top of the pile. Repeat this again after another few days and again a few days later. Your flowers will take up to six weeks to dry, although some things will be usable after just two or three weeks.

ARTIFICIAL FLOWERS

No longer the rather nasty, tatty items found in cheap cafés, most artificial flowers are fabulous imitations of their fresh counterparts. You can now choose from a huge range of fabric (called silk, although they are often not), plastic or parchment. Generally, silk flowers are cheaper than parchment, but the latter have an irresistible quality which silk are unable to match. Virtually every flower is represented artificially, which is great if you want to find daffodils in October. When mixed with fresh or dried flowers, they can be almost indistinguishable from the real thing, especially if viewed from a distance.

Artificial flowers are easy to handle, last indefinitely and because they have improved so much in recent years, are a floral designer's delight. Also available is a large range of fabric, parchment and plastic foliage, some of which is a superb copy of nature, and ideal for making garlands, headdresses and decorating gifts.

MAKING GARLANDS

Many florists and all floral wholesalers will sell a wide range of wreaths. These vary from the rounds of dry or fresh florist's foam, through vine and twig wreaths to wire garland rings. Or make a base from twigs or chicken wire.

CHICKEN WIRE RINGS

These are either filled with sphagnum moss (for dry arrangements) or wet foam (for fresh ones). Take a long thin rectangle of chicken wire and wrap it around a fat wad of moss or pieces of florist's foam ①. Twist the wire edges in on themselves and then mould the wire into a circle (working around your waistline is a good guide). When you have formed your circle, secure the two ends together with some stub wire ② (see picture overleaf).

WREATH RINGS

These are sturdy wire bases which are usually covered with sphagnum moss. The moss is secured to the base by winding florist's string or twine round and round the ring to hold it in place.

❶

❷

AFFIXING FOLIAGE AND FLOWERS TO A GARLAND

What you add to a garland base is entirely up to you. Usually, a foundation of foliage is inserted first ④ and other items, such as cones, berries or flowers are added on top. If you are using a wet foam wreath, it is simple to push the stems of the plants directly into the foam. For any other type of wreath using dried or artificial plants, you can either push the wired ends of the items into the base, or stick on the pieces with a glue gun.

FOAM RINGS

Made in different sizes, foam rings are also made from dry or wet foam.

TWIG OR VINE WREATHS

These are very popular and look great even without anything on them. They are inexpensive to buy, but you can make your own, particularly if you are interested in basket making. Supple twigs are simply twisted around each other and secured into a ring with some heavy gauge stub wire. If you don't want a natural coloured base, you can paint it by rubbing emulsion paint on to the twigs with a cloth ③. If you buy a painted wreath, you can distress it slightly by sanding the surface with a small piece of sandpaper.

WIRING CONES AND SEEDHEADS

Although a glue gun is immensely handy for many garland designs, occasionally it is necessary to attach a piece to a length of wire. This is especially so for fresh arrangements, where glue is inappropriate.

To wire strange shapes such as cones or seedheads, take a piece of medium gauge stub wire, bend the end into a U-shape and hook it around the base of the piece ⑤. Once the wire is hooked in place, twist the shorter end around

❹

❸

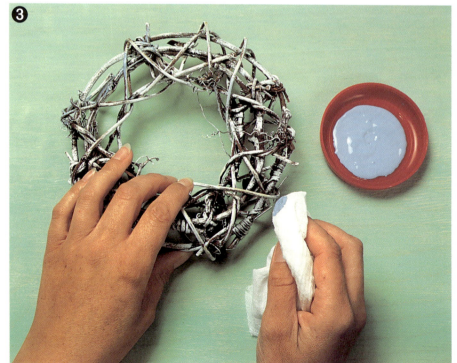

❺

⑥

HANGING A PENDANT OR GARLAND

Make a hanging loop with heavy gauge stub wire. Push one end of wire through the top of the garland or pendant and twist the wire back on itself to secure. Push through the other end of wire a little distance away and repeat ⑧. This secure hanging device should not show when the design is in place.

MAKING POSIES AND BOUQUETS

A posy can be a simple gathering of garden flowers or a more formal display, swathed in tissue paper and cellophane

the longer piece to give you a tail ⑥ which you can then insert into florist's foam or a twig wreath base.

ADDING FRUIT

The easiest way to secure fruit into an arrangement is to spear it with a wooden skewer or cocktail stick ⑦ and push this into florist's foam. If you are working on a garland, swag or pendant and glue is inappropriate, wire fruit by pushing in a piece of heavy gauge stub wire (in much the same way as you do for cones or seedheads). Twist the wire around to secure it and pull it hard so that most of the wire sinks into the flesh of the fruit and then disappears.

⑧

with a mass of shiny ribbons. Whatever type of posy or bouquet you make, here are a few simple presentation tips to help you.

BUILDING UP A BUNCH

When you are assembling your flowers, it helps to build up a small bunch first, securing it with some floral tape ① (see picture overleaf) before adding more flowers to build up the display.

Most florists use string or floral twine, but I have always found the stretchy floral tape to be much easier to use. You only need a short length (no more than around 20 cm [8 in]) at a time. Then, to use the stretchy tape, pull it tightly and you will find the tape will cling in place neatly.

⑦

1

STEM ENDS

For a natural finish, leave the stem ends of a posy showing, but make sure they are all neatly trimmed to the same length. For fresh posies or bouquets, it helps to preserve the flowers by covering the ends with a piece of cellophane or plastic wrap and then tissue paper. This prevents the ends from drying out too quickly and also provides a neat finish for any sap-oozing stems in the bouquet.

Cut a small square of cellophane or plastic wrap, fold around the end of the stems and secure with a rubber band ②. Cut a slightly larger square of white or coloured tissue paper, place the stem ends in the centre of the tissue and fasten with another rubber band which you can then cover with gift ribbon ③.

FORMAL BOUQUETS

Don't be daunted by these more elaborate floral displays: the key is the finishing touches, like the ribbon flourish and clear floral cellophane. Buy both ribbons and cellophane from a floral supplier, although you can improvise with giftwrap ribbon from stationery stores. The flamboyant bows which usually decorate these floral masterpieces are simplicity itself, and are merely pull-up devices, needing zero skill to operate.

You can either make up your display directly on to the cellophane and then wrap it around the flowers (working either so that the cellophane is wrapped around the sides of the piece, or so that it folds over at the top of the display), or you can make up your arrangement on a worksurface and then envelop it in the cellophane.

Secure the cellophane at the base with a small piece of narrow gift ribbon. Tie this tightly and finish with a knot. This is then covered with a larger display bow and ribbon.

As a finishing touch, run a piece of matching wide ribbon up the side of the cellophane, or even along the top, and secure with staples. Add ripples of narrower ribbon over the top of the wide ribbon to cover the staples, sticking it in place with double-sided tape and curl any tail ends of ribbon with a scissor blade.

2

LILIES

These fabulous florist's favourites look and smell utterly divine. However, the pollen from the exotic looking stamens is absolutely indelible and will stain furniture and clothes. It will also blemish the petals if they are brushed against. Because of this, many florists trim off the stamen ends before arranging lilies. Do this using a small pair of scissors. Hold the flower upside down so that the pollen falls off on to a scrap of paper ④.

3

④

MAKING BUTTONHOLES

To make successful buttonholes, you must invest in the green paper tape used by professional florists. This tape is slightly stretchy and will cling to itself once it has been wound round the stems of the buttonhole. It also gives a neat finish and covers any wire you might have used.

Cut one or two flowers to length (hold them against your chest to give you a more accurate idea of the length that you need). You might also, perhaps, hold a tiny piece of foliage as well ①. Secure together with a twist of reel wire, then cover the ends with the green paper tape ②. Finish with a little coordinating ribbon.

MAKING TREES

Little mop-head or cone trees covered with moss, foliage or flowerheads are a popular gift idea and they are very easy to make. You will need a suitable pot, twigs or small branches for the trunk and a florist's foam shape (sphere or cone) for the head. Depending on the size of the tree, it can be fixed into the pot in dry florist's foam, soft clay or even set in plaster of Paris.

Hold up the pot, trunk and tree top to gauge the proportions; make sure the sizes work together and that the pot is not too big for the head or vice versa ①. Wedge florist's foam or soft florist's clay into the pot, push in the trunk (a thick and thinner piece together often look quite stylish) and squash the sphere or cone head down on top. If you are making a large tree, it is stronger if you set the trunk into plaster of Paris. You will need to fill the pot with crumpled newspaper and then a plastic bag. Pour the plaster into the plastic bag and insert the trunk. You will need to support the trunk until the plaster sets.

Decorate the tree head with flowers or leaves ② (a glue gun really comes into its own here) and pack some lichen or bun moss around the base of the trunk to cover the foam, clay or plaster.

❶

❶

❷

❷

MAKING RIBBONS

There are so many lovely ribbons
available that it is sometimes difficult
to choose just one.

PAPER RIBBON
Don't confuse this type of ribbon with
the floral paper ribbons described
below. It is actually much more
expensive and is a relatively recent
newcomer to the floral scene. It is sold
in coils, often available by the metre
(yard). As it is twisted round on itself,
you will have to tease it open to use it.
It is available in a wide choice of
colours, particularly the duskier shades.

SATIN RIBBON
Most frequently used for dress-making
or other crafts, satin ribbon is widely
available from department stores, fabric
shops and market stalls, and makes an
excellent finish for many floral designs.
However, it isn't as manageable as
traditional floral ribbons.

TRADITIONAL FLORAL PAPER RIBBON
This is one of the cheapest ribbons to
buy. It is available in a wide colour
range, including a vast array of pastel
shades. It is usually sold in 2.5 cm
(1 in) widths and as the narrow 5 mm
(¼ in) gift ribbon. Also available in
pull-up bows, this type of ribbon can be
bought from any floral supplier or
well-stocked florist.

WIRED RIBBON
Like satin ribbon, wired ribbon is also
fabric ribbon which has a very fine wire
stitched into both edges. This means
that any bow or flourish will retain its
shape. Wired ribbon often comes in
lavish colours and patterns, many with
a metallic tinge or glint.

MAKING A BOW
Fold a length of ribbon into a bow
shape and hold together with your
fingers ①. Wind a snippet of reel wire
around the centre of the bow to hold it
in place ② and cover with a small piece
of ribbon. Secure at the back with a
piece of sticky tape.

If you want curling ribbon ends
(only achievable with paper gift
ribbon), so popular with giftwrapping,
pull the sharp side of a scissor blade up
and along the ribbon in one quick
movement ③.

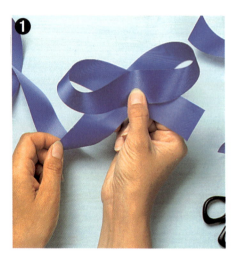

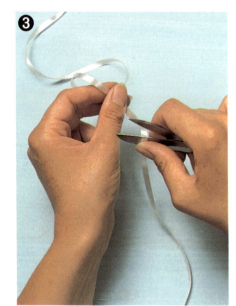

OTHER TECHNIQUES

I have always thought of flower
arranging as such a narrow term, and
instead have constantly tried to push
back the boundaries of how flowers and
plant material of all types can be
incorporated into other aspects of home
style. It is great fun to experiment and
combine flowers with other traditional
craft techniques such as decoupage,
stamping and other forms of decoration.
After all, flowers and foliage have been
decorative forms since decoration
began, so don't feel limited to flowers in
baskets, bunches or vases.

For those unfamiliar with some of
these other techniques, I have given
basic instructions here, although
excellent books on each of these skills
exist if you want to venture further.

PAPIER MÂCHÉ
This is such a cheap and cheerful craft,
and one which has grown in popularity
recently. Its naive form has a particular
charm, although practised artists can
achieve such sophisticated effects that
papier mâché can resemble pottery.

Basically, soft, gluey paper is applied
to a mould and built up in layers which,
when dry, is strong and durable. The
papier mâché is then painted and
varnished to finish off.

Use newspaper, torn into tiny strips,
and dip them into a solution of flour
and water paste (the consistency of

unwhipped cream). The mould to which you apply the paper strips can be cardboard (as in the case of the napkin rings on page 50 and opposite, bottom right ①), wire, clay, a bowl or a balloon. Generally, the first two types of mould stay in place when the papier mâché is complete; the latter three·are removed when the papier mâché is dry, leaving you with a paper shell. Any mould which is being removed should be coated with petroleum jelly first to prevent the papier mâché from sticking.

Build up the layers (three or four is usually sufficient) and leave to dry thoroughly before giving a coat of white emulsion paint. You are then ready to decorate as you wish.

STAMPING

This form of decoration is so simple, yet can be so effective. A stamp can be made from all manner of materials: cork, sponge, rubber, wood. The stamp is pushed onto an inked stamp pad or is painted with a layer of water-based paint before being stamped onto the item to be decorated.

Rubber stamps can be bought in hobby shops, stationers or through mail order suppliers. There are many floral motifs available. Alternatively, wooden textile printing blocks make excellent stamps and many come in floral designs, too. I used textile blocks to print the pretty potpourri bags below ②, along with a simple daisy stamp carved from a wine cork. Although you can use many

items to create stamps, floral devices are usually best bought or carved with a sharp craft knife from cork or polystyrene.

STENCILLING

Many people are familiar with this form of embellishment, which has a big place in home decoration. Making your own stencils are easy and fun. Use clear acetate or stencil card. Trace, copy or draw your design onto some paper and transfer to the stencil material (for acetate, you can simply lay the design underneath and cut out the shape from that; card needs to be drawn on with a felt-tipped pen). The motif is cut out using a sharp craft knife. The stencil is then taped onto the item to be decorated and paint is either dabbed, crayoned, brushed or sprayed onto the stencil. When dry, the stencil is

removed and the motif will appear underneath.

Stencilling is a great way of achieving a regular repeat pattern (see the stencilled pansy pots below ③), and you can also use other household items as stencils such as lace or doilies. For example, see the Rose Frame on page 74 where doilies create a pretty edge.

Specialist stencil shops or DIY stores will sell stencil paints, crayons, pre-cut stencils, card and acetate, although the basics can also be bought from stationers.

DECOUPAGE

This is a craft much loved by the Victorians who applied it to screens, trays and other furniture. Today, it has seen something of a revival, and once again, it is not just the traditional technique which is being employed, but other styles and variations which are broadening this craft and bringing it to a much wider audience.

Traditionally, decoupage involves cutting out pictures from books and magazines, sticking them onto any object in an attractive pattern, and sealing with several layers of glossy varnish.

In *Floral Gifts*, I have combined pressed flowers with this traditional technique (see Decoupage Card, page 68 and below ④) for a very unusual and delicate effect.

Use a paper glue, such as PVA and an acrylic varnish for most items.

BOUQUETS, POSIES AND GARLANDS

These are the traditional floral gifts. A bouquet for a birthday, a garland for Christmas, a posy to say 'thank you'. In this chapter, you can see just how easy it is to make a formal bouquet or a pretty presentation posy packed in net and tissue in a matching gift box. Or try your hand at a garland: there are no rules here, and you'll find a variety from which to choose.

WINTER GARLAND

Parchment flowers are perfect for winter garlands. They do not fade or wither, and look really elegant in almost any setting. These creamy, green peony roses are set on a white painted vine wreath against fake cotoneaster foliage and teamed with gilded paper figs and dried orange slices. It's a pleasure to have this garland hanging at any time of year, but it makes an unusual and refreshing change at Christmas.

1 If you can only buy a natural vine wreath, paint it white first with emulsion paint. Once dry, rub the wreath with a piece of sandpaper to distress the surface and reveal some of the natural wood that is beneath.

YOU WILL NEED

White painted vine wreath
Sandpaper
Secateurs or scissors
Fake cotoneaster foliage
Reel wire
White parchment peony roses
Gold paint
Fake figs
Glue gun
Dried orange slices and tiny oranges
Heavy gauge stub wire

— VARIATIONS —

For a more traditional garland, use fake fur or pine foliage with gilded cones, clusters of artificial berries and bright red, silk poinsettias.

2 Using secateurs or scissors, cut the foliage into manageable pieces and twist them in and out of the wreath, working in one direction only, until the base is virtually covered. Make sure that you reveal some of the white wreath base though. Use lengths of the reel wire to keep the foliage in place.

3 Trim down the peony roses using secateurs or wire cutters and push the stems into the wreath. Keep the flowers at an equal distance apart, and peel open their petals once they are in position. (Parchment flowers are packaged with the petals and leaves tucked in. It's terrific fun to mould and tweak these into shape: they are much more manageable and obedient than their fresh cousins!)

4 Put a little gold paint on your finger and rub on to the fake figs to add highlights. Cut down their stems with wire cutters or secateurs and slot into the display. I have only used two bunches to add a change of texture and interest to the garland.

5 Finally, plug in the hot glue gun and once the glue has melted, stick the dried orange slices and small dried oranges in place around the wreath. Hot glue sticks rapidly, so work quickly. If you make a mistake, pull the piece off immediately, as items can be quite difficult to remove once the glue has dried. Create a hanging loop at the back of the garland with the stub wire (see page 13).

FORMAL BOUQUET

Virtually everyone is delighted to receive a traditional style bouquet, and it is really not at all difficult to make one which can look every bit as professional as that ordered through a florist. The secret is the finishing touches: the shiny clear wrapping and flamboyant ribbons. Select your flowers with care. To some extent, this is a matter of choice, but a well-coordinated colour combination always looks chic and elegant.

1 Lay the roll of clear florist's wrap on to the worksurface and carefully unroll it, until you have enough to work on. The width of the clear wrap will determine the height of the arrangement. Do not cut the clear wrap at this stage. Begin making your arrangement by placing the first few pieces of foliage and irises on the clear wrap, leaving sufficient on either side of the display so that you will be able to completely enclose the flowers. Only cut off the stem ends when you are happy with the position of the flowers. Make sure that they are all cut level at the bottom.

YOU WILL NEED

Roll clear florist's wrap
Foliage
Purple irises
Secateurs
Purple and cream scabious
Yellow roses
1 m (1 yd) narrow florist's ribbon
Scissors
1 m (1 yd) wide florist's ribbon
Stapler
Florist's bow
Double-sided tape

— VARIATIONS —

Try other colour combinations: orange lilies, yellow gerbera and purple lizianthus for a really tropical look, or burgundy chrysanthemums with cream coloured spider chrysanthemums and deep red roses for a rich and opulent bouquet.

2 Build up the display using the purple scabious. Add a few cream coloured ones to highlight the arrangement, then begin to place the roses further down the display. (The yellow roses pick up the colour of the brilliant stripe in the iris flowers.) Continue adding the roses until the arrangement looks complete.

3 Tie the bouquet with a scrap of the narrow gift ribbon and knot firmly. Ensure you have plenty of clear wrap on either side of the bouquet, then cut it from the roll. Pleat up the clear wrap around the base of the bouquet, making sure it forms a gentle series of folds on each side. Tie neatly and firmly with another scrap of the narrow gift ribbon. Measure out a length of wide gift ribbon along one edge of the clear wrap and neatly staple into place with the staples running parallel to the flower stems.

4 It is difficult to achieve the wonderful bows that adorn these types of bouquets without some degree of effort, so take a tip from the professional florist and use a pull-up florist's bow. They are inexpensive, totally effortless and yet still add that spectacular flourish. Pull up the fine ribbons on the bow and the whole thing will magically pop into shape. Use these fine ribbons to tie the bow to the bouquet and curl the trailing ends with a scissor blade (see page 16).

5 To finish, place a piece of narrow gift ribbon along the edge of the wider ribbon and secure in place at each staple with a thin strip of double-sided tape. As you stick the ribbon down at each staple, allow the ribbon to ripple into gentle folds.

PRESENTATION POSY

Everyone is delighted with a posy of flowers, and this particular one will arrive in pristine condition as it is packed in a customized gift box. Hat boxes are now widely available in a range of different sizes from stores selling greetings cards and stationery. If you don't like the pattern on the box, recover it with pretty giftwrap or wallpaper to complement the flowers. Pack with shredded tissue before adding the posy.

1 Strip the leaves from the lower stem ends of the roses and remove any nasty thorns. Group together several stems, interspersing them with the brodiaea, and secure with florist's tape.

YOU WILL NEED
Pink roses
Blue brodiaea
Florist's tape
Scissors
Ruscus foliage
Purple net
Gift ribbon in lilac and deep purple
Purple tissue paper

TIP

It is nice to cover the standard gift boxes, as you can achieve a perfect match with your flowers. PVA glue is suitable for most papers. Add a pretty bow on the box lid for a final flourish.

2 Add in some ruscus stems, making sure that you strip off any lower leaves, so that the posy comes together tightly. Bind the posy together just beneath the flower heads with a strip of florist's tape.

3 Continue to build up the posy, creating an even mix of roses, brodiaea and foliage. When you have added the last pieces, secure with a final piece of tape.

4 Cut a piece of purple net into a rectangle, twice the height of the posy and long enough to wrap around it with generous folds. Wrap the net around the flowers, securing it at the stems with some of the lilac gift ribbon. Tie the ribbon in a tight knot but leave the ends trailing for the time being.

5 Cut the tissue paper into three large leaf shapes. Take one shape at a time and pleat at the base with your fingers. Place the tissue leaves around the posy and bind with the deep purple gift ribbon. Tie the ribbon in a tight knot and leave the ends trailing. Curl the four ribbon ends using a scissor blade (see page 16).

HERB GARLAND

The ideal gift for the enthusiastic cook, this fabulously fragrant herb garland can be plucked and plundered during the winter months to add savour to dishes. However, as it is such a welcome decorative addition to any kitchen, you might find friends loathe to destroy your gift, but instead resort to storecupboard jars!

1 Slowly roll up the mesh into a sausage shape, stuffing it with the sphagnum moss as you work. Mould the mesh as you roll it to create an evenly thick shape.

YOU WILL NEED

Small sheet of plastic-coated wire mesh

Sphagnum moss

Selection of freshly-dried herbs

Reel wire

Bay leaves

Chilli peppers

Garlic

Medium gauge stub wire

Hessian ribbon

— VARIATIONS —

This garland contains culinary herbs, but why not make one for the bedroom of bathroom with herbs renowned for their therapeutic qualities: lavender, rosemary, sage, chamomile and lemon balm?

2 Wrap the sausage shape wire into a small ring, securing the ends together by intertwining the ends of the wire. Make sure that you do this thoroughly to prevent it from unravelling later on.

3 Tie the herbs into small bundles with reel wire, leaving sufficient wire to secure the bundle to the garland. Work up one side of the garland first, and then the other, covering the wire with the next bundle as you go. (The bound ends at the top of the garland will be covered by the ribbon at the end.)

4 Continue to build up around the garland with the herbs until it is entirely covered. Then add the bay leaves and chilli peppers in the same way, scattering them around the garland.

5 To secure the garlic to the garland, take a piece of medium gauge stub wire and form a small hairpin bend at one end. Push the longer piece of wire through the garlic, allowing the hairpin shape to slice into the garlic and disappear below its skin. Use the remaining tail of wire to attach the garlic to the garland. Finish with a bright hessian ribbon tied into a loose bow.

BOUQUETS, POSIES AND GARLANDS GALLERY

Lavender posy

For a posy which is scented as well as decorative, gather together a neat bunch of pretty little sunray (helipterum) and surround them with a well-ordered circlet of heady, fragrant lavender. Keep the flower heads level and trim the stems to the same length for a smart finish. Secure with twine or tape and cover with purple ribbon and decorative twine.

Summertime hat

A little straw hat makes such a pleasing wall hanging. Wind narrow ribbon around the crown and leave overlong tails hanging, then trim with a circle of bright yellow strawflowers (helichrysum), sticking the flower heads in place with a glue gun.

Gerbera bouquet

The vivid colours of gerbera always ensure a cheerful composition. Mix just four gerbera with a few daisy chrysanthemums and leather leaf fern for an informal but attractive bouquet. Finish with a frill of tissue paper and forest green satin ribbon.

Mini cherry garland

Tiny twig wreath bases are inexpensive to buy and can be speedily transformed into a welcome present. Twist around checkered black and white ribbon, then wind a narrower red ribbon around on top. Slot in a bunch of fake cherries and leaves and add a red ribbon tied in a loose bow at the top.

Sunflower plait

Plaited corn makes an excellent base for flower ropes and garlands. If you are unable to obtain enough stalks to plait your own, corn plaits are readily available to buy. Secure the ends at the top with heavy gauge stub wire and add a jaunty parchment sunflower, wedged into the plait.

Delphinium wreath

Wreaths look stunning when composed of just one flower. Cut the dried delphinium flower heads into 12.5 cm (5 in) lengths. Push row upon row of them into a dried foam base, flatten each row against the base and tie them down at their tops with a piece of reel wire. Work around the wreath in one direction and finish with glossy purple ribbon in a loop at both top and bottom.

29

BASKETS AND POTS

Have fun with inexpensive terracotta pots, which can be decorated in a huge number of different ways. Spray paint, colour rubbing or simple poster paints can all transform the humble garden pot into a delightful and unexpected gift. And once you've enjoyed painting and stencilling, fill the pots with miniature plants, fresh flowers or candles trimmed with dried flower heads. Baskets, too, offer numerous possibilities for floral gifts and there are a great many delightful baskets available in every conceivable size and shape.

STENCILLED PANSY POTS

Decorated pots make such a versatile and welcome gift. They are really fun to do, and once you begin, you will find it hard to stop! These inexpensive terracotta pots have been painted, colour-rubbed and stencilled with little pansy motifs. For other decorative ideas, see the Gallery on pages 40-1. Stationery shops should sell the acetate for the stencil, while most DIY or decorating stores will stock stencil crayons.

1 Paint each terracotta pot both on the inside and outside with a coat of the cream coloured emulsion paint. Leave to dry.

YOU WILL NEED

Terracotta pots

Emulsion paint (cream)

Paintbrush

Old lint-free rag

Acrylic or emulsion paints (green, purple)

Tracing paper

Pen

Thick cardboard or cutting mat

Acetate

Craft knife

Stencil crayons (purple, yellow)

Fine paintbrush

Artist's acrylic paint (green)

—— VARIATIONS ——

If you don't like potted plants, fill the pots with soaked florist's foam and create a small fresh flower display. Alternatively, pack with dry foam and dried or silk flowers. Silk pansies look especially effective.

2 Dab the old lint-free rag into a small amount of green acrylic or emulsion paint and rub on to the pot. Do not rub the paint all over, just here and there and work quickly as the paint dries while you rub. Now add a few touches of purple. If the colour is too strong, rub over a little cream coloured emulsion until you are happy with the effect.

3 Trace off a pansy shape using the photograph here as a guide, or use a picture in a gardening catalogue or book. Keep the shape bold and simple; do not be tempted to include small details. Place the tracing on the thick piece of cardboard or cutting mat and place a small piece of the acetate over the top. Cut out the shape from the acetate using the craft knife.

4 Hold the stencil in place on the pot with your fingers. Then, using the other hand, dab some of the stencil crayon on to the cut-outs. Rub the paint into the cut-out with your finger, keeping the stencil pressed down against the pot. Lift up the stencil to reveal your motif. Now repeat around the pot at regular intervals. When the motifs are complete, use the other colour crayon to make a dot in the centre of each flower.

5 Using the fine paintbrush, paint a little green leaf motif to link the pansy flowers. Fill with your favourite potted plant: perhaps pansies!

—————————— TIP ——————————

It is worth marking out the position of each motif with a pencil first to ensure you have a regular pattern and do not end up with an uneven gap, or two motifs butting up to each other.

FLOWER AND FRUIT BASKET

A basket brimming with fresh fruit is always a well-received gift, but why not make something a little more special by bedecking the basket itself with clusters of dried flowers. Long after the fruit has been eaten, the basket can continue to be enjoyed.

Bear in mind that the larger the basket, the more dried flowers you will need to use. Don't skimp on the flowers though, as the effect will be spoilt. If your budget can't quite stretch to a basket of this size, make a smaller version (see Variations below).

1 Begin by gathering together little clusters of flowers and seedheads. Keep the clusters small, but don't cut the stems too short. Secure the clusters with a length of reel wire that is about 15 cm (6 in) long. Wind the wire around the stems two or three times and attach the cluster to the basket with the remaining tails of wire, tying them firmly in place.

YOU WILL NEED

Dried peonies
Dried *Nigella damascena*
Dried gypsophila
Dried pink roses
Secateurs or scissors
Reel wire
Dried lavender
Florist's tape
Paper ribbon
Medium gauge stub wire

——— VARIATIONS ———

If you like this idea, but want to scale it down, try smaller baskets and fill them with little fruits such as grapes, lychees, plums or berries. Instead of wiring on dried flower clusters, stick flower heads and leaves to the basket rim with a glue gun.

2 Continue to form little flower clusters and wire them around one side of the basket, always securing them so that the flower heads face the same way. Build up the display, covering the wired stems of each cluster with the heads of the next small bunch.

3 To add depth and contrast to this design, use small bunches of lavender. The deep blue-mauve is the perfect foil to the soft pinks and creams of the other flowers. When you reach the end of one side, neaten the wire by winding some florist's tape over the top.

4 When you have completed both sides of the basket, make a small cluster of flowers and tape them to the handle (tape is more stable than wire at this point). This gives the design a little continuity. You will cover the tape with the bow, but keep it as neat as you can.

5 Paper ribbon must be teased apart before it can be used. When you have a sufficient length, fold it into a bow shape and wrap a piece of stub wire around the centre to secure it. Don't cut off the wire tails as these can be used to attach the bow to the handle. Finish off the bow by wrapping a smaller piece of ribbon around the centre to cover the wire. Cut the tails of the bow into deeply angled swallow's tails.

IVY TOPIARY

Classical topiary has adorned stately, landscaped gardens for centuries. Usually sculpted from the glossy-leaved box, skilful gardeners have created an amazing array of shapes ranging from cones and spheres to birds and even figures.

The poor man's counterpart to this wonderful art is ivy topiary, where this ubiquitous plant is trained around wire forms to emulate its box and privet cousins. A challenge to make, these charming models are easy to keep trained into shape and serve as a really unusual gift for the garden lover.

1 Cut the chicken wire into a rectangle (around 60 x 30 cm [2 x 1 ft]) and roll into a loose sausage shape. Bend the wire in two places to form the tail and the neck of the bird. (Always use gloves when handling chicken wire: you get a much better grip and you will not snare your fingers on any jagged ends.)

TIP

Buy a well-established ivy (almost any variety will work well), with long trailing stems, as you will achieve the topiary shape without having to wait for the plant to grow.

2 Mould the chicken wire to create a head and trim off the other end so that a tail is formed. Gently pull apart the wire in the centre to create a plumper shape for the body.

3 Unless you are lucky enough to buy a plant in an attractive pot, ease the ivy out of its plastic container and repot into a terracotta pot, adding more compost if necessary. Gently tease apart the trailing stems, so that each one hangs separately.

4 Wedge a length of the bamboo stick into the wire shape and secure it with a little stub wire to prevent it swivelling about. Push the stick into the centre of the soil and push down the soil firmly.

5 Wind the ivy stems up and around the wire shape, working from both sides. Secure in places with little pieces of wire to maintain a regular shape. Continue to assess the shape as you work, and trim off any really rogue leaves which ruin the line. Remember to work down the head to form a beak. Finally, tie the stems around the base of the stick with green twine to define the shape and hold the ivy in place. Use the same twine to decorate the top of the pot.

TABLETOP CHRISTMAS TREE

It is hard to believe that when the life of the humble poppy is over, exotic and sculptural seedheads come from the same plant. As the most exciting part of the seedhead is the fabulous star-shaped tip, it is worth showing this off to its best advantage — a mini Christmas tree makes the perfect opportunity to do this, as the pretty stars all face outwards from a central cone.

1 You might be fortunate enough to buy dry foam in a small enough cone-shape, but generally, most cones are a little too large for this project and need to be pared down using an old, long-bladed kitchen knife. Remember that the poppy heads are quite large and will make the final shape a lot bigger than you might imagine. Experiment a little first if you're not sure. When you have a suitably sized, rough cone shape, paint it with a pale colour emulsion paint. Leave to dry.

YOU WILL NEED

Small block of dry foam or foam cone

Long-bladed kitchen knife

Emulsion paint (white or cream)

Paintbrush

Terracotta pot

Gloss or enamel paint (dark green)

Florist's clay

Bamboo cane

Two or three bunches of natural poppy seedheads

All-purpose glue

Tartan ribbon

Stub wire

Silver or clear glitter spray

VARIATIONS

You can use other seedheads for this project — *Nigella*, for example — or try the tiny cones available from most floral suppliers. These do not need to be wired into the foam, but instead can be stuck on with a glue gun. For a more glitzy effect, spray the whole tree with silver, gold or copper paint, then add ropes of pearls or glittering stars.

2 Paint the terracotta pot with the same emulsion paint to act as a primer then, when dry, coat with dark green gloss or enamel paint. Leave to dry. Squash some soft florist's clay into the base of the pot and cut down a piece of garden bamboo cane which will anchor the cone into the clay.

3 Sort the poppy heads into different sizes; the larger ones will form the base of the tree. Cut the poppy heads down so that the stems are really short (around 2.5 cm [1 in]) and, to make it easier to insert them into the foam, cut them at an angle. Begin by slotting the larger seedheads in around the base of the tree, butting each one up to its neighbour.

4 Begin to work up the tree, graduating the poppy heads, so that you begin with the larger ones and finish with the smaller ones at the top. For the neatest finish, work up the cone in straight lines from the base. Although it may not work exactly, you will achieve a more uniform finish. At this stage, you can swap about the seedheads to achieve the best effect, but once you are happy with the overall shape, remove the heads, one at a time, add a dab of glue and push back into the foam.

5 Use narrow strips of tartan ribbon and form into little bows. Wrap a piece of stub wire once around the centre of the bow, and twist the wire tails together to secure them. Add the bows to the tree at random. Give the whole tree a spray with the silver or clear glitter spray and finish with a little tartan ribbon wrapped around the pot.

BASKETS AND POTS GALLERY

Fresh flower basket (bottom)
Miniature baskets are inexpensive and plentiful, and make fabulous gifts when filled with a selection of fresh flowers. Pack the basket with wet florist's foam before adding the flowers: we've used September asters and cornflowers.

Spring basket
Whatever the time of year, you can have spring in your home. This pretty wire basket has been filled with sphagnum moss and a selection of silk, spring flowers. Wedge the flowers into a layer of florist's soft clay packed into the bottom of the basket.

Gilded tree
This classical tree stands in a golden pot, made simply by spraying a flowerpot with gold spray paint. Cover a dry florist's foam sphere with fake ivy leaves, spraying just a few with gold to add highlights.

Wall basket

Another pretty variation for a miniature basket, this little wall hanging is packed with wet florist's foam and filled with daisy chrysanthemums, currant foliage and cornflowers. Pack a little plastic wrap into the base of the basket to prevent the water from the foam dripping down the wall.

Poppy pot

For a really long-lasting display, you cannot beat parchment flowers which will last and last and only fade in the strongest of lights. These flamboyant poppies surround a column of dried green barley. Use dried florist's foam in the pot. Strands of raffia are tied around the pot for a complementary finish.

Candle pot

Paint the pot in sections with poster paints over a coat of white emulsion, using masking tape to achieve the straight lines. Wedge florist's soft clay into the pot before adding the dried flowers.

Star pot

Terracotta pots are so inexpensive to buy and they can be decorated in numerous ways. This one has been painted first with white primer and then simple star stencils were applied before a coat of blue poster paint was added. To achieve the lovely mottled effect, give the pot the faintest mist of spray adhesive before adding the blue paint.

41

TABLE DECORATIONS

Whether you decide to make a table decoration to take to your host, or something to enhance your own table which your guests can later take home with them, you will find something in this chapter to inspire you. Don't feel that flowers are reserved for a centrepiece either, use them on napkins, as cutlery ties, mix them with candles or try your hand at frosting fresh blooms to make individual place settings.

CANDLE RING

No special dinner would be complete without a spectacular centrepiece. Candles are a traditional favourite, and these tall yellow ones sit in a garland of shiny foliage, bright, crisp flower heads and mouthwatering lemons and limes. Candle rings are popular in many cultures, the circle signifying friendship. Although a fabulous piece, this candle ring should not take you more than an hour to put together.

1 Cut a long rectangle of chicken wire (this one was about 60 x 30 cm [24 x 12 in], although you can make this larger or smaller) and place small blocks of wet foam along its length, like a little train. Fold the wire lengthways into the centre, twisting the raw edges together to secure it. Wear the gloves when doing this as the wire is quite sharp.

YOU WILL NEED

Chicken wire
Secateurs or wire cutters
Wet florist's foam
Gardening gloves
Few stub wires
Stems of foliage
Scissors
3-4 lemons
3-4 limes
Cocktail or orange sticks
White daisy chrysanthemums
White spider chrysanthemums
Floral candle holders
Three yellow candles

TIP

If you are unable to buy floral candle holders, buy plain flat ones, made either from glass or metal, and set them against the inner edges of the garland, tucking them well into the foliage so that the bases are covered.

2 Twist the wire and foam sausage into a circle, moulding it against your waist for a rounded effect. Join the two ends with some stub wires and adjust until you are happy with the circle. Begin to add short pieces of foliage, pushing the stem ends into the wet foam and working around the ring in one direction only.

3 When the wire is virtually covered both inside and out with foliage, add the fruit. These can be used whole or cut in half. Push each piece on to a cocktail or orange stick and push the stick firmly into the foam.

4 Add clusters of chrysanthemums into the arrangement, cutting their stems short and pushing them into the foam. Work around the circle in the same direction as the foliage.

5 Finally, add the candle holders. Floral candle holders have spikes so that you can push them into the foam. Set them around the ring, equidistantly and then pop the candles in place and light.

TABLE BOUQUETS

These draping bouquets are quite simple to make and fix to any type of table. They last well out of water, yet transform a dinner or buffet table into a veritable feast for the eye. And the really nice thing is that your guests can take one home with them: any slightly weary flowers will quickly revive in a long drink of water. For the best results, keep the made-up bouquets in water until just before your guests arrive.

1 Lay the three protea down on a worksurface to form the basic hanging shape. When the heads are in place, cut the stems to the same length with secateurs or strong scissors.

YOU WILL NEED

3 protea
Secateurs or strong scissors
Deep pink alstroemeria
Florist's tape
Heavy gauge stub wire
Tassel
Shiny ribbon
Medium gauge stub wire

--- TIP ---

These type of draping displays look very dramatic set against a fabric swag. Simple to make, a swag will also create an excellent means by which to hang your bouquets.
Take a narrow length of contrasting fabric, a little longer than the side of the table. Twist the fabric gently and wind with a little gold or decorative cord. Secure at intervals along the table edge, either with panel pins or — on a good piece of furniture — sew on to the main tablecloth with strong buttonhole thread. The bouquets are then hooked into the swag at these points.

2 Place two or three stems of alstroemeria on top of the protea to fill out the shape. Then bind them together neatly with a little florist's tape to secure and carefully trim off any overhanging stem ends.

3 Now lay two or three more alstroemeria along the length of the bouquet so that the flower heads conceal the stems already in place. This will also fill out the display. Check the bouquet against the table edge until you are satisfied with the look of the piece and then secure it with a piece of florist's tape

4 To form the hook from which the arrangement will hang, take the heavy gauge stub wire and push it up under the tape as shown in the picture above. Push the wire through about halfway, then bend both ends back into two hook shapes.

5 Loop the tassel on to the hooks and attach the whole to the edge of the table (see the Tip on the opposite page). Tie a lavish bow with the shiny ribbon and attach to the front of the bouquet with the medium gauge stub wire. Make sure that the fixings and tape are covered by the ribbon.

SANTA FE TROUGH

Freshly dried flowers may seem a contradiction in terms but, in fact, just-dried flowers still retain a richness of colour and form which those that have been sitting around for many months do not have. If you are lucky to be able to grow your own flowers for drying, consider the three specimens here as likely candidates. They all dry easily in the air and the rich, warm colours are hard to beat.

This pretty trough, with its little slot-in trays, makes an ideal table centrepiece, and it was this that inspired the choice of flowers. It is the perfect gift to take to a host, or something to make for your own dinner party.

1 Mould a 2.5 cm (1 in) layer of the florist's soft clay into the base of the trough. Push in the candle holders, positioning them equidistantly in the trough.

YOU WILL NEED

Small trough or similar
Florist's soft clay
Floral candle holders
Dried yarrow
Dried safflowers (*Carthamus*)
Dried eryngium
2 blue candles

TIP

It is worth having two or three sets of candles so that you can replace them as they burn down. Do take care, though, as dried flowers are flammable. Never allow the candle to burn down too far. Always extinguish it and replace when the flame is within 2.5 cm (1 in) of the flowers.

2 Measure the yarrow against the side of the trough and cut down the stems so that it fits into the trough and just hangs over the edge. Make a line of yarrow all around the edge of the trough.

3 Trim down the safflowers in the same way, taking care as they (and the eryngium) are painfully spiky. Then create a regimental line of flower heads sitting neatly behind the row of yarrow. Work along one side of the trough, and then the other.

4 Now add a second, slightly taller row, of safflowers behind the first, and place two or three flowers at each end of the trough so that there are no obvious gaps.

5 Cut down the eryngium in the same way and intersperse them fairly randomly throughout the display. Finally, insert the candles.

TABLE DECORATIONS GALLERY

Leafy cutlery ties

Break away from traditional place settings by tying each guest's cutlery with a trailing stem of fake foliage. You could also adapt this for napkins, too.

Jewelled napkin rings

Gold *Nigella* seedheads have been cut in half and glued to a napkin ring made from cut cardboard tubes wound with string and painted in purple, silver and gold.

Miniature iced cakes

A truly lovely gift — you can make one cake for each guest to take home with them. Cut a larger cake into smaller pieces, ice and add iridescent ribbon and frosted violets or scented geranium leaves to decorate.

Christmas nut star

A glossy addition to the Christmas table: wire is shaped into a star and studded with gold and silver nuts, leaves and cones.

Pressed flower napkin rings

These napkin rings are made from papier mâché which has been painted with emulsion paint. Pressed flowers and leaves have been glued into place and the ring has been varnished for protection.

Carnation ties

Fake silk and parchment carnations look almost better than the real thing. Sew them on to check ribbon to create a chic and elegant napkin or cutlery tie.

Floating flowers

Ever popular, quick to assemble and long-lasting, this table centrepiece shows off the pretty heads of the gerbera to their best advantage. Creamy coloured floating candles complete the display.

WEDDING FLOWERS

If friends are planning a wedding, why not offer to help with the flowers as your wedding gift? Almost every wedding is celebrated with a lavish and exuberant display of flowers: to decorate the church, the reception area, the cake, the wedding car and, of course, there are those worn and carried by the bride and bridesmaids. On the following pages you will find ideas for every aspect of this most joyous of occasions, from scented rose petal confetti to a spectacular wedding pendant.

BRIDE'S HEADDRESS

*Whether the bride decides to wear a
traditional veil or not, flowers make the
perfect headdress. As fresh flowers seldom
stand the test of time, or a warmly radiating
head, choose silk versions, which are now so
enchanting they almost look better than the
real thing. Try to buy silk flowers which
have been dusted with powder to give them a
softer, more authentic appearance.*

1 Silk flowers are often sold in clusters, with
several flower heads and leaves grouped on
one stem. These are easy to pull apart to give you
individual flowers and smaller leaf clusters. Use
secateurs, strong scissors or wire cutters to trim
down the stems.

YOU WILL NEED

Silk flowers in cream, plum and deep burgundy

Secateurs, strong scissors or wire cutters

White headband

White florist's tape

Pearl clusters

All-purpose glue

Lapsana or gypsophila

TIP

To be really sure that your design is working, fit your
headband on to a large doll or wig stand before you begin
adding the flowers. Attach the flowers with small bits of
sticky tape, which you can lift off and stick down as much as
you want until you have a design with which you are happy.

2 Begin to lay the flowers — one or two at a time — against the headband and secure them with tape. Use quite small lengths of tape to secure just two or three stems. Keep the tape as neat as possible; although it is unlikely to show, it should look perfect for that most special day.

3 Work around the band, adding the flowers and leaves in small groupings. Occasionally intersperse a deep coloured flower for contrast. Gently slip the band on to your own head and check your progress. Adjust the floral arrangement accordingly until you are pleased with the result.

4 Pearl clusters are sold in small posies by floral suppliers. Untwist the paper which binds them and separate out into smaller groups. Add these at intervals around the band by pushing them into the tape which is already holding the flowers (add a small dab of glue if you wish).

5 Finally, soften the design with wispy stems of Lapsana or gypsophila. Lapsana is probably the better choice as the flower heads are really tiny and more delicate. Insert these into the headband in the same way that you added the pearls. A small dab of glue is probably advisable here, but avoid using a glue gun which can leave messy, spider's-web trails.

BRIDAL POSY

For a country-style wedding, choose a hand-gathered posy of sapphire blue cornflowers and crisp, white marguerites. This type of informal posy has grown in popularity over recent years, yet it is as ancient as time itself. The stems of the posy are bound with hopsack ribbon, which continues the country theme, yet is a practical hand-hold for sticky, nervous hands. Keep the posy in water until just before the wedding, then blot the ends with kitchen paper before binding.

1 Gather a cluster of cornflowers for the centre of the posy, keeping the flower heads level. Secure the stems with florist's tape and trim the ends of the stems level.

YOU WILL NEED

Cornflowers
Florist's tape
Marguerites
Kitchen paper towel
Hopsack or linen ribbon

—— VARIATIONS ——

Other excellent country-style combinations include wheat, cornflowers and fake poppies (real ones will not last); Queen Anne's lace, cream full-blown roses and lady's mantle (*Alchemilla mollis*) or simply masses of mixed or single-colour sweetpeas.

2 Build up around the cornflowers with a thick layer of marguerites. Work round and round in a circle and keep assessing your progress. When you are happy with the result, bind with some more florist's tape. Don't cut off too much tape at a time — around 20 cm (8 in) is usually sufficient.

3 Place a few cornflowers around the outer edge, adding some of the lovely, wobbly-stemmed buds to soften the outline of the posy. Bind with tape and trim all the stem ends neatly. Leave in water until you are ready to depart for the ceremony.

4 Blot the stem ends with kitchen towel and bind with some natural hopsack or linen ribbon. For a neat finish, lay a piece of ribbon along the length of the stems as shown, fold over at the top at a right angle, and begin to wind around the stem until just 2.5 cm (1 in) of stem ends are showing.

5 Tie the ribbon into a loose bow and leave the ends hanging down. Trim the ends at an angle with sharp scissors to finish.

WEDDING PENDANT

Weddings are the perfect excuse for spending just a little extra on fresh flowers to create one or a pair of floral pendants. They can be hung at the entrance to a church or, for civil ceremonies, used to decorate the room where the celebrations will be held. A pendant can be made in advance and transported to the venue; however, it is probably much easier to assemble it in situ on the morning of the wedding.

1 Soak the foam well but ensure it is not dripping. Lay the two pieces of foam on to a rectangle of chicken wire end to end and twist in the wire, securing the sharp ends (wear the gloves for protection). Mould the wire around the foam until you have a long, rectangular shape. Add a heavy gauge piece of wire at the top to serve as a hanging loop (see page 13).

YOU WILL NEED

2 bricks of fresh florist's foam

Gardening gloves

Chicken wire

Heavy gauge stub wire

Yellow lilies

Cream roses

Pale orange lilies

Deep apricot roses

Eucalyptus foliage

Gypsophila

Exotic seedheads

Emulsion paint (cream) (optional)

Cream paper ribbon

Medium gauge stub wire

— VARIATIONS —

I've used rich golden yellow and deep apricot, highlighted with cream, but you could try other colour schemes. Pink 'Stargazer' lilies with roses in shades of pink; deep orange lilies offset with orange and peach coloured roses; or cream 'Madonna' lilies with cream and pale yellow tea roses for a purer look would each look equally good.

2 Turn the shape over and lay on to the worksurface. Now form a loose 'S' shape with the yellow lilies, cutting the stems short and using flower heads that are open and unblemished. (Remember to snip off the stamens first, see page 14 for more details.)

3 Fill in around the lilies with sprays of cream roses and some of the pale orange lilies. Keep the stems of the lilies short, but the rose stems can be a little longer to form the small sprays. At this stage, it is probably better to hang the pendant in place so that you can assess the display as you work.

4 Continue to build up the design with sprays of apricot and cream roses, filling in around the sides and base with foliage. To define the shape of the pendant, create a curving spray of apricot-coloured roses at the base.

5 Tuck in small pieces of the eucalyptus foliage to fill in any gaps, then soften the whole display with clusters of wispy gypsophila. Finally, to add a little interest, wire up a few unusual seedheads (see page 12) and slot these into the arrangement. I dabbed these with a little cream-coloured emulsion paint first to help them blend more harmoniously with the bridal colours. Tie some paper ribbon into a generous bow and attach to the top of the pendant with a piece of stub wire.

SCENTED WEDDING ALBUM

A really novel and unusual gift for the bride and groom is this beautiful, fragrant photograph album covered in a delicate floral paper. Fill the album with photographs you or a friend has taken on the day for a truly special present that is guaranteed to outlive many others.

1 Dry the petals as described on page 10. Cover one side of one piece of tissue with the spray adhesive and gradually tip the petals on to the surface spreading them as evenly as possibly all over the sheet.

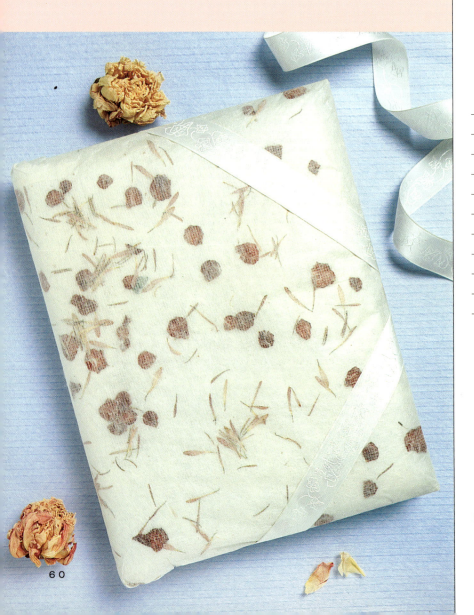

YOU WILL NEED

Selection of dried petals

3 sheets of handmade tissue paper

Spray adhesive

2 boards (optional)

Photograph album

Wadding

Double-sided tape

Pastel coloured paper

Large paper bag

Rose-scented potpourri

Satin ribbon

VARIATIONS

For the most delicate and exquisite effect, invest in handmade paper (this isn't as expensive as you might think). Floral paper can be used for many things: giftwrap is perhaps the most obvious, but you could turn it into framed pictures, potpourri or gift bags, or a lampshade covering.

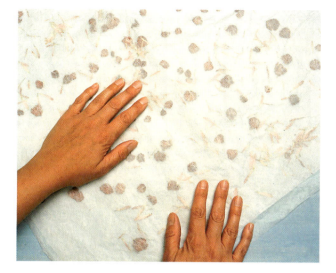

2 Place a second piece of the tissue paper on top of the first and smooth it out with your hands. Although it isn't vital, it does help if you flatten the paper down between two boards for a day or two.

3 Cut the wadding into three pieces, two rectangles to cover the front and back of the photograph album and a long strip for the spine. Attach to the album with double-sided tape. Then cover the album with the remaining piece of tissue paper, securing it to the inside of the album cover with double-sided tape.

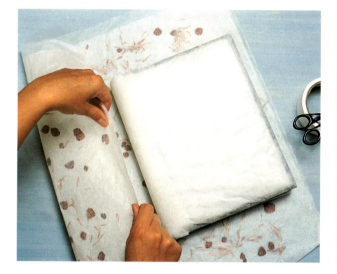

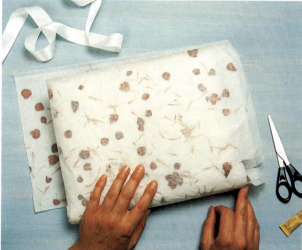

4 Lay the covered album onto the floral paper, and wrap the paper around, again securing it to the inside with double-sided tape. Trim the corners to avoid any bulkiness.

5 To neaten the spine, cut the paper up towards the spine and tuck in behind the spiral binding, securing it with a little glue. Cut two pieces of pastel-coloured paper and stick to the inside of the cover at the front and back; these will form end papers and will cover any untidy bits. Place the completed album in a sealed bag containing some of the rose-scented potpourri and leave for at least a week. The potpourri will impregnate the album with fragrance. Fill the album with pictures of the happy day and bind one or two corners with creamy satin ribbon.

WEDDING FLOWERS GALLERY

Rose petal confetti (below)

Dried rose petals are possibly the most romantic choice to scatter over the bride and groom. Dry as described on page 10 and add a few drops of rose essential oil to a bag of the petals a week or so before the wedding.

Silver horseshoe

A traditional gift for the bride which she can carry with her after the ceremony. Decorate a bought silver horseshoe with tiny dried pink rosebuds and gypsophila. Add the narrowest cream silk ribbon.

Heather buttonhole

An alternative to the traditional buttonhole favoured by men at wedding gatherings. Heather is, of course, the ideal choice for a Scottish (or those with Scottish roots) wedding. Tie with a piece of tartan ribbon

Fresh flower boules

A lovely alternative to posies, these flower boules can be carried by bride or bridesmaids alike. Simply stud a soaked foam sphere with chrysanthemum flowerheads and wire in a hanging loop of ribbon.

Purple buttonhole

Suitable for men or women, this purple buttonhole is made from long-lasting scabious and statice. Tie with a simple cream satin ribbon.

Wedding corsage

A wedding corsage is very popular and here, creamy alstroemeria are wrapped in white tulle and finished with a satin bow.

Bridesmaid's hair circlet

Every bridesmaid — particularly the younger ones — long to look like princesses on the wedding day, and this romantic dried and fake flower hair garland is fit for the finest. Florist's wire is twisted into a circlet and covered with fake ivy foliage, cream and pink lace, peonies and deep red rosebuds. Use a glue gun rather than wire.

CARDS AND KEEPSAKES

Use flowers to embellish gift tags, candles, greetings cards, picture frames or presentation boxes. You will not need many flowers, just one or two thoughtfully placed pieces can transform many an everyday item into something which the recipient will want to cherish for months or years to come. As well as using actual flowers and leaves, there are also crafty ways with floral motifs to enhance your gift.

HERB CANDLES

Pure white candles decorated with fresh herbs make a lovely gift, especially if you package several together. Although you can buy excellent candle making kits, these ones are made with household candles and use ordinary kitchen utensils. You don't need to press the herbs before using them, although it is worth avoiding succulent varieties or those with large, hairy leaves.

1 Cut the herbs into small, manageable pieces which you feel will make an attractive design around the candle. (Try to select smallish, feathery or flattish leaves, as they are easier to work with.)

─── **TIP** ───

Experiment with some old candles first, until you are confident with the candle dipping. As the whole candle is not being dipped, an unsightly ridge can form unless you twirl the candle quickly and deftly in the hot wax. It is not that tricky, but it's worth practising once or twice first.

─── **VARIATIONS** ───

For a more colourful design, stick pressed flowers on to the candle instead of herbs.

2 Apply a squiggle of glue to the candle and gently press the herb into place. Use a cocktail or orange stick if your fingers become too sticky. Work your way around the base of the candle, sticking the herbs into place. Set to one side to dry.

3 Chop up at least ten household candles with the sharp knife. Don't worry about removing the wick. This can be fished out later when the wax has melted.

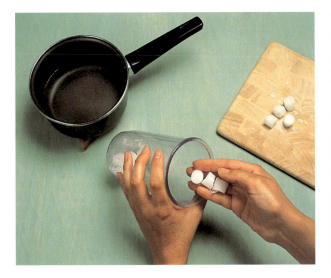

4 Tip the candle pieces into the heatproof bowl or jug and place in a saucepan of simmering water. Keep the water simmering at a very low heat until all the wax has melted. This can take quite a time (at least half an hour) and you may need to top up the boiling water to prevent the pan from drying out.

5 When all the wax has melted, fish out the bits of wick with the slotted spoon. Hold the heatproof container with an oven mitt or cloth, and tilt it at an angle. Lower the decorated candle into the wax and quickly twist the candle in the wax to coat the herbs. You do not need to cover the whole candle. One quick coating of wax seals in the herbs and gives them an attractive translucent layer.

DECOUPAGE GREETINGS CARDS

Decoupage is an enjoyable craft in itself, but when combined with pressed flowers and leaves, it takes on a unique style. You do not need to use a flower press: cardboard and several heavy books will work just as well, and the flowers and leaves take about ten days before they are ready to use. Card blanks are readily available from arts and crafts suppliers. You could make a whole pack of cards, pack them in a pretty box and present them as a gift in their own right.

1 To make your flower press, cut some pieces of the corrugated cardboard and tissue into manageable sized pieces which will fit comfortably in between the heavy books you plan to use. The books must be larger all around than the cardboard, otherwise flowers on the outer edges will not press properly. You will need two pieces of cardboard and two pieces of tissue for each press. Assemble the leaves and flowers and lay them neatly on to a sheet of tissue with a small space between each one.

YOU WILL NEED

Corrugated cardboard

Tissue

Several heavy books

Sharp scissors

Selection of flowers and leaves (try pansies, cow parsley, ivy leaves)

Cut-outs from magazines, books, giftwrap

Card blanks

PVA glue

Cocktail or orange sticks

Craft knife

Gold spray paint (optional)

Acrylic varnish

— VARIATIONS —

The cards shown here have been designed to look classical yet delicate, but you could adapt the idea to make really contemporary cards using flowers and leaves which have a strong shape, combining them with bolder, more modern cut-outs.

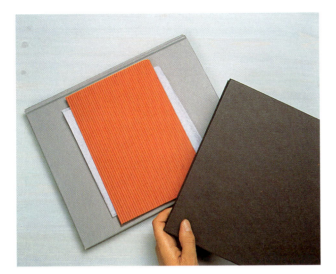

2 Place another piece of tissue on top of the piece holding the flowers, making sure that none of the petals or leaves have wrinkled or buckled and place the tissue sandwich in between the two pieces of cardboard. Now place the whole thing in between two large, heavy books. After three or four days, put two more books on top of the pile, and repeat this after another two or three days. You will find that most flowers will be ready in about ten days, but you might need to wait a little longer for some specimens.

3 Cut out a selection of images from the magazines, books, and giftwrap. Cut them very neatly with the sharp scissors and stick on to the card blank with the PVA or other paper glue. Build up a background design ready to add the flowers and leaves.

4 Add the pressed flowers and leaves one at a time using the cocktail or orange stick to help you position them. Flowers, in particular, will be very fragile and petals can tear really easily, so be as careful as possible. Apply tiny blobs of PVA glue to the backs of the flowers and leaves, using a cocktail or orange stick. Stick them carefully into place.

5 Leave the card to dry out completely and then turn it over to the back and trim around all the edges with the craft knife for a neat finish. If you wish, you can then add a border to the card using the gold spray paint. To do this, mask off the card using a large scrap of cardboard and spray one edge of the card with paint. When that edge is dry, spray the next edge. Wait for this to dry, then repeat the process on the other two edges, masking off the main part of the card while you do so. For added protection, apply a fine coat of acrylic varnish. When the card is completely dry, place it between some heavy books to flatten it.

BABY GIFT

Every new mother — however weary — is delighted with a gift of flowers. Why not combine a little present for the baby along with some fresh flowers? Here, pale lilac scabious and apricot hued roses sit against a backdrop of pure white lizianthus — colours which are suitable for either a new baby boy or girl. A cheerful teddy peeks from the little basket like a pilot in a hot air balloon. He can be removed from the basket later and placed in the crib along with the newborn.

1 Make sure your teddy fits neatly into the basket, even if he has to kneel down. Then tuck the teddy bear's bottom half into a clean plastic bag to prevent him from becoming soiled by the florist's foam.

YOU WILL NEED

Teddy bear
Basket
Plastic bag
Fresh florist's foam
White lizianthus
Purple scabious
Apricot coloured roses
Ruscus foliage
Satin ribbon

VARIATIONS

Although I haven't shown this here, there is no reason why you shouldn't swathe the whole basket in clear florist's wrap and tie with a white florist's bow or matching spotty satin ribbon.

2 Pack a small tablet of the soaked florist's foam into the basket. Then build up an outline of lizianthus, following the line of the basket handle, but making sure that the flowers do not create too wide a display.

3 Insert stems of scabious in front of the lizianthus, cutting them down so that they are a little shorter than their white neighbours. In front of these, place a few roses; once again they should be a little shorter still. Make sure you leave room for the teddy bear in the front of the display.

4 Finish off the floral arrangement, by filling in any gaps with ruscus stems. This will add contrast and depth to the lizianthus, scabious and roses, adding some much-needed greenery.

5 Finally, tie a loose floppy bow on the basket handle and carefully tuck teddy inside ready to be presented to mother and baby.

POTPOURRI BOX

This is a floral gift that should appeal to either sex. The wooden box has been stained and painted with a small motif before being given a lustrous gilt edge. It has been filled with a woody, lemony potpourri. If you feel freehand-painting is a little daunting, why not stamp or stencil a design on to the lid instead? I found these little boxes in a bargain shop, but you could re-use cigar boxes or ones containing natural cosmetics.

1 Sand down the box all over and then stain it with a coat of the wood stain, painting it on both inside and out; this one is antique pine. Leave to dry completely.

YOU WILL NEED

Wooden box
Sandpaper
Wood stain
Paintbrush
Sharp HB pencil
Paper
Poster or acrylic paints
Spray paint (gold)
Varnish
Potpourri mix: ½ cup each of golden mushrooms, chilli peppers, orange and lemon peel, small dried oranges, bark, star anise
1 tbsp coarse salt
½ tbsp mixed spice
3 cloves
2 drops lemon essential oil

TIP

Dried bark, wood shavings, dried oranges and other dried seedheads are often sold in mixed bags from floral suppliers. These mixes are usually inexpensive and will probably provide you with the basis for your potpourri.

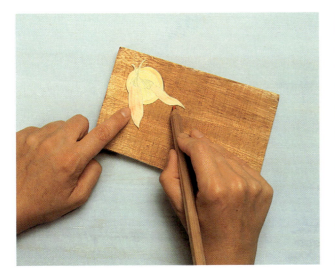

2 Draw your required motif on some paper first, following the photograph here as a guide. Then cut it out and draw around it on the box lid. Remove the paper and draw in the rest of the motif with pencil.

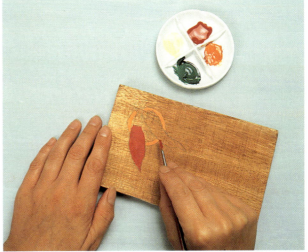

3 Carefully paint the motif with the poster or acrylic paints, washing the paintbrush meticulously when changing colours. Leave the motif to dry thoroughly before moving onto the next step.

4 Mask off the lid with a scrap of paper and spray with gold paint to create a wonderful gilded rim (see step 5 on page 69 for more details on how to do this). Seal the box with varnish and leave to dry.

5 Mix all the potpourri ingredients together in a large mixing bowl. Add the drops of essential oil and stir well. Then transfer to an airtight container and leave to cure for four to six weeks, when it will be ready to decant into the wooden box.

ROSE FRAME

This is such a pretty way to use dried roses, and makes a lovely gift for a female friend or relative. You can decorate an old picture frame in any way you choose, but here I have stencilled a lacy design using a paper doiley. As most picture frames are not deep enough to take the flowerheads, you will need to create a slightly deeper back — which is simple enough to make from a scrap of cardboard.

1 Remove the backing to the frame and discard. Sand down the frame carefully and coat both back and front with white emulsion paint to act as a base for the enamel paint. When the emulsion is dry, paint the front of the frame with the enamel and leave to dry.

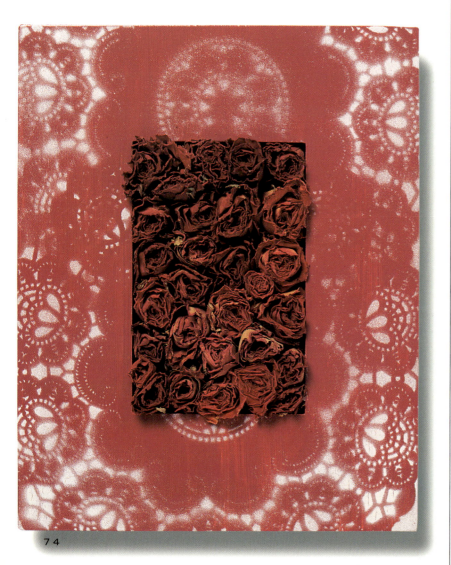

YOU WILL NEED

Old picture frame

Emulsion paint (white)

Paintbrush

Enamel hobby paint (deep pink)

Two or three paper doilies

Masking tape

Spray paint (white)

Cardboard

Pencil

Ruler

Eraser

Craft knife

Scissors

Dried roseheads

All-purpose glue or glue gun

--- TIP ---

Roses are quite expensive to buy dried, but you can buy bags of dried roseheads (often used for potpourri) quite cheaply. These are ideal for this type of project.

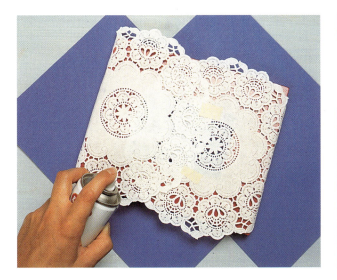

2 The number of doilies that you need for this part of the project will depend on the size of your doilies, but two overlapping, as here, will provide an all-over pattern. Tape the doilies down with the masking tape and spray the frame with the white paint. Leave to dry before removing the doilies.

3 Place your prepared frame onto a piece of cardboard and mark out the the inner rectangle or square (depending on the shape of the frame, this one has a rectangular opening) with a pencil. Remove the frame and measure 10 mm (⅜ in) all around the first rectangle and draw this in too, as shown. Finally, draw another rectangle 5 mm (¼ in) out from the previous one. Erase the innermost rectangle, as it is no longer needed.

4 Cut out the rectangle with the craft knife, using the outermost line as your cutting line. Now score along the inner lines using a scissor blade. Fold along the lines to create a shallow box. Cut out the corners so that the box folds neatly then stick in place on the back of the frame with masking tape. Trim and stick the tape as tidily as possible. If you want, you can spray the back of the frame white to keep everything really neat.

5 Place the roseheads in the recess you have created, butting them up neatly and making sure they are as flush as possible with the surrounding frame. As you work, glue the roseheads in neat rows using a glue gun for a really speedy result (although all-purpose glue is perfectly adequate).

CARDS AND KEEPSAKES GALLERY

Gift boxes

These little bought gift boxes have been embellished with pretty silk sunflowers and anemones. Cut the flower heads off with scissors and glue gun the flowers to the lids and sides.

Greetings cards (below)

Pressed leaves are arranged on a card blank and then covered with a piece of tissue paper so that they are revealed in silhouette. Decorative ribbon adds the finishing touch. Or use leaves as a stencil and spray with metallic paint.

Toiletries tidy

Encapsulate flowers between layers of clear PVC and machine with brightly-coloured stitching. Then fold into three and tie with some decorative cord. Secure each floral device with hot glue.

Wheatfield picture frame (below)
Decorate a picture frame with sisal string and dried wheat and finish with two or three stalks wound with raffia.

Potpourri bags
These pretty bags are made from giftwrap stamped with old floral textile printing blocks. For a floral finish, tie with silk foliage or dried flowers.

Gift tags
Make your own tags by sponging some paint on to plain card, adding a pressed flower or leaf and a ribbon tie in the corner.

USEFUL ADDRESSES

Contact your local florist for fresh flowers, florists' tape, florists' wire, dried moss, and small baskets and pots. Many florists and craft shops stock silk and dried flowers, or will order these for you. Also consult the Yellow Pages for stockists of dried, silk and paper flowers in your area.

UNITED KINGDOM

Dried Flowers

Country Style
358 Fulwood Road
Ranmoor
Sheffield S10 3GD
Tel: 01742 309067

Lesley Hart Dried Flowers
37 Smith Street
Warwick CV34 4JA
Tel: (01926) 490356

Hartwood Aromatics
12 Station Road
Hatton, Warwick
Tel: (01926) 842 873

The Herbal Apothecary
103 High Street
Syston, Leicester
Tel: (01533) 602 690

Hilliers Garden Centre
Woodhouse Lane
Botley
Southampton S03 2EZ
Tel: (01489) 782306

The Hop Shop
Castle Farm
Shoreham
Sevenoaks, Kent
Tel: 01959 523 219

Terence Moore Designs
The Barn Workshop
Burleigh Lane
Crawley Down
West Sussex RH10 4LF
Tel: (01342) 717 944

Robson & Watley Ltd
2A Pembroke Road
Bromley, Kent
Tel: (0181) 466 0830

Veevers Carter
The Chelsea Gardener
125 Sydney Street
London SW3
Tel: (0171) 352 7658

Silk Flowers

Artificial Plant Company
164 Old Brompton Rd.
London SW5 OBA
Tel: 0171 835 1500

The Chelsea Garden
125 Sydney Street
London SW3 NR
Tel: 0171 352 5656

The Flower Barn
37 Hill Lane
Barnham
West Sussex PO22 0BL
Tel: (01243) 553 490

The Flower Loft
Brewers Loft
E4 Marabout Ind. Est.
Dorchester
Dorset DT1 1YA
Tel: 01305 251 853

The Silk Plant Contractors
Co.
1 Cole Rd.
Watford.
Tel: 21 01 82

Suppliers

Ascalon Design Parchment
Flowers
The Coach House
Aylesmore Court
St Briavels
Glos GL15 6UQ
Tel: 01594 530567

Fast Flowers Ltd
609 Fulham Road
London SW6 5UA
Tel: 0171 381 6422

Prices Patent Candle Co Ltd
110 York Road
London SW11 3RU
Tel: 0171 228 2001

Specialist Crafts Ltd
PO Box 247
Leicester
LE1 9QS
Tel: 0116 251 0405

Warmadams Nurseries
Cattlegate Road
Crews Hill
Enfield
Tel: 0181 363 1928

NETHERLANDS

Star Dried Flowers BV
Floralann 2A
PO Box 101
2230 AC Rijnsburg

W Hogewoning BV
Floralann 2G
PO Box 265
2230 AG Rijnsburg
Tel: (31) 1718 28501

SOUTH AFRICA

Anne's Arts and Crafts
6 Recreation Road
Fish Hoek
Cape Town
Tel: (021) 782 2061

Auckland Park Floral
Boutique
7 Seventh street
Melville
Johannesburg 2092
Tel: (011) 726 2116

Hiningklip Dry Flowers
13 Lady Anne Avenue
Newlands
Cape Town 770
Tel: (021) 64 4410

Penny Lane Potteries
233 Marshall Street
Johannesburg 2001
Tel: (011) 334 6058

Peter's Florist
54 First Avenue
Durban 4001
Tel: (031) 309 3439

Polyflora
8 January Road
Bloemfontein
Tel: (051) 34 1371

Price & Sons (Pty) Ltd
23 Francis Street
Woodstock
Cape Town 7925
Tel: (021) 45 4201

AUSTRALIA

Bonds Nursery
277 Mona Vale Road
Terrey Hills NSW 2084
Tel: (02) 486 3222

Dominion Agencies
20 Stuart Road
Dulwich
SA 5065
Tel: (08) 332 6688

Dryflora Australia
3 Plowman Street
Olinda
VIC 3788
Tel: (03) 751 2324

Flowerama
Unit 27
8 Gladstone Road
Castle Hill
NSW 2154
Tel: (02) 680 2320

Flower World
12 Sara Grove
Tottenham
VIC 3012
Tel: (03) 315 2388

Hawkins Home and Garden
623 Albany Creek Road
Albany Creek
Queensland 4035
Tel: (07) 264 1022

Newmans Nursery
North East Road
Tea Tree Gulley
South Australia 5091
Tel: (08) 264 2661

Petal Pushers
Cnr Dandenong and
    William Roads
Prahran
Victoria 3181
Tel: (03) 9510 4196

Timbertop Nursery
1387 Wanneroo Road
Wanneroo
Western Australia 6065
Tel: (09) 306 3398

Valley View Flowers
104 Gavour Road
Wattle Gorve
WA 6107
Tel: (09) 453 668

NEW ZEALAND

Auckland Flower
Wholesalers Ltd
388 Church St.
Penrose
Tel: (09) 579 5692

Colleen Murphy Florists
119 Akitchener Road
Milford Square
Tel: (09) 489 5961

Expression Flower Shop
359 Gt North Road
Henderson
Tel: (09) 836 5068

The Florist Group
Auckland City
Tel: (09) 366 7016

Flower Systems Ltd
8 Macklehurst Road
Auckland
Tel: (09) 337 4515

Headerish Flowers
Shirley
Christchurch
Tel: (0800) 50 505

Interflora
Head Office
Tel: (0800) 80 88 80
(Branches nationwide)

Palmers Gardenworld
44 Khuber Pass Rd
Auckland
Tel: (09) 302 0400

Reumuera Florist, The
319 Reumuera Road
Auckland
Tel: (09) 520 8379

INDEX